This Journal Belongs To

LOVE
YOURSELF
KNOW
YOURSELF

A 90-Day Self-Discovery Journal

LILIAN O. EBUOMA MD

Copyright © 2026 Lilian O. Ebuoma, MD
All rights reserved. This book or parts thereof may not be reproduced in any form, stored in any retrieval system, or transmitted in any form by any means—electronic, mechanical, photocopy, recording, or otherwise—without prior written permission of the author, except as provided by United States of America copyright law.

ISBNs:
Paperback   979-8-99-164015-2
Hardcover   979-8-99-164016-9

First Edition

Book Production by Hal Clifford Associates
www.hcabooks.com

By reading this document, the reader agrees that under no circumstances is the author or the publisher responsible for any losses, direct or indirect, which are incurred as a result of the use of information contained within this document, including, but not limited to, errors, omissions, or inaccuracies.

Legal Notice:
This book is copyright protected. Please note the information contained within this document is for educational and personal use only. You cannot amend, distribute, sell, use, quote or paraphrase any part, or the content within this book, without the consent of the author or publisher.

www.lilianebuoma.com
Cape Girardeau, Missouri 63701

Disclaimer

This journal is designed to provide inspiration, reflection, and personal growth guidance. It is not a substitute for professional advice. This journal is not intended to replace professional medical, psychological, or therapeutic advice, diagnosis, or treatment. If you have any health or mental-health concerns, please consult with a qualified healthcare provider. Individual results may vary. The reader is responsible for their own emotional and psychological well-being. Participation in the exercises should be at your own discretion and comfort level. This is a private and confidential journal. The author and creators of this journal are not responsible for any breaches of confidentiality or privacy. The quotes, affirmations, and guidance provided in this journal are based on various sources and philosophies. They are intended for educational and inspirational purposes only. The accuracy, completeness, and relevance of the information are not guaranteed. By using this journal, you agree to hold harmless the creators, authors, and publishers from all claims arising from your use of the content. All content, including but not limited to quotes, affirmations, prompts, and exercises, are protected by copyright laws. Unauthorized reproduction, distribution, or commercial use of this material is prohibited without prior written consent from the creators. By using this journal, you acknowledge that you have read, understood, and agreed to the terms and conditions outlined in this disclaimer. Your journey of self-discovery and self-love is a personal endeavor, and we wish you all the best on your path to greater understanding and fulfillment.

The two most important days in your life are the day you are born and the day you find out why.

—*Mark Twain*

The Transformative Power of Self-Discovery

Self-awareness, self-acceptance, self-affirmation, self-advocacy, and self-love form the foundational pillars of self-discovery and development. These elements are not mere steps but crucial components of a transformational journey toward a fulfilling, meaningful, and authentic life. Self-discovery is a process of observation, exploration, careful inventory, and curation of "Your Own Uniqueness": YOU. It involves looking inwardly, accepting what is found, and using it to become who you aspire to be. This is the essence of growth, renewal, and self-actualization.

An optimal state of being is the most important nurturing environment you can inhabit. *For as within so without.* Living and functioning from this state is entirely within your control and solely your space to cultivate and achieve through self-discovery. Self-discovery is a lifelong responsibility and practice that infuses your life's journey with meaning and deep personal power.

Finding meaning and your life purpose requires focus and direction, which requires clarity, and clarity begins with first knowing who you are. If you do not define yourself, others and society will readily impose on you their versions of who and what they think you should be based on their perspectives, expectations, and beliefs.

The quest for self-actualization means you are perpetually engaged in the process of self-creation. The outcomes of this depend on how deeply and courageously you love and own who you are and how devoted you are to honoring your core values. As the Greek poet Pindar advised, "Become who you are by learning who you are." The first move toward this clarity is inward. Excavate and explore what lies beneath the mask, façades, and fences for a deeper understanding and connection with self.

You will find a masterpiece, who is fearfully and wonderfully made! The world needs your unique essence for the significant impact only you can make. Love and knowledge of oneself are the beginnings of making you and the world a better place.

Introduction

Welcome to your 90-day guided journey of self-discovery. In this journal, you will explore the transformative power of LOVE: Learning, Ownership, Validation, and Expansion of self as pillars for discovering, embracing, and nurturing your true self. This journal is designed to take you on a transformational voyage toward embracing your true essence and cultivating a deep sense of love and compassion for yourself.

Each day, you will embark on a journey of self-reflection, growth, and understanding to support your growth and cultivate a deeper sense of self-love. Through mindful reflection, gratitude practices, and mindset-shifting questions, you will follow a path of personal growth, inner harmony, and discovery. It is best to go through this journal in order over a 90-day period, but feel free to begin based on where your mind leads.

Section 1:
LEARNING

"Knowing yourself is the beginning of all wisdom."

—Aristotle

DAY 1

Date: ....

I embrace the journey of self-discovery and trust the process of unfolding who I truly am.

Who am I? And why am I here?

....
....
....
....
....
....
....
....
....
....
....

How do I want to be remembered, and what legacy do I wish to leave behind?

....
....
....
....
....
....
....
....
....
....
....
....

"The only person you are destined to become is the person you decide to be."

—Ralph Waldo Emerson

DAY 2

Date: _____

> *I trust that the journey of self-discovery will reveal the beautiful, authentic me.*

What are the beliefs I hold about myself, and how do they shape my identity?

_____
_____
_____
_____
_____
_____
_____
_____
_____
_____

What is my life's purpose, and how can I live in alignment with it every day?

_____
_____
_____
_____
_____
_____
_____
_____
_____
_____
_____

"Your task is not to seek for love, but merely to seek and find all the barriers within yourself that you have built against it."

—Rumi

DAY 3

Date:

I am a source of infinite creativity, love, and wisdom.

How do I practice forgiveness and compassion toward myself when I make mistakes?

_____
_____
_____
_____
_____
_____
_____
_____

What limiting beliefs and thoughts have I internalized, and how do they impact my self-perception?

_____
_____
_____
_____
_____
_____
_____
_____

"The journey of self-discovery begins with self-love."

—Shannon L. Alder

DAY 4

Date: _____

> *I am deserving of love, acceptance, and understanding as I discover who I am.*

Clarity begins by first knowing who you are. What aspects of myself do I appreciate the most, and why?

What does self-love mean to me, and how can I cultivate it more deeply in my life?

"The way you treat yourself sets the standard for others."

—Sonya Frie

DAY 5

Date:

I am patient and gentle with myself as I uncover my true essence.

In what ways can I show gratitude toward my past, present, and future self?

How will I honor the wishes of my desired future self?

"You are not a drop in the ocean. You are the entire ocean in a drop."

—Rumi

DAY 6

Date:

I am a unique and powerful being, embodying the vastness of the universe within me.

How can I better appreciate my own significance and worth?

How can I fully embrace and embody the limitless potential within me?

"Your visions will become clear only when you can look into your own heart. Who looks outside, dreams; who looks inside, awakes."

—Carl Jung

DAY 7

Date: ....

My true visions emerge from deep self-reflection and understanding.

What truths have I discovered about myself when I take the time to look within?

_____
_____
_____
_____
_____
_____
_____
_____
_____

How will my life change if I commit to regularly looking inside for clarity and awakening?

_____
_____
_____
_____
_____
_____
_____
_____
_____

"Be yourself; everyone else is already taken."

—Oscar Wilde

DAY 8

Date:

My self-discovery leads me to a life of purpose, passion, and fulfillment.

What aspects of myself do I still struggle to fully embrace and express?

What beliefs or fears are holding me back from showing up as my true authentic self in all areas of my life?

"To be yourself in a world that is constantly trying to make you something else is the greatest accomplishment."

—Ralph Waldo Emerson

DAY 9

Date:

I am proud of who I am and what I have achieved.

What aspects of my identity do I sometimes hide, and why?

What steps can I take to cultivate a deeper sense of self-acceptance, self-worth, and authenticity?

"Your time is limited, don't waste it living someone else's life."

—Steve Jobs

DAY 10

Date:

I respect the values of others while staying true to my own.

In what ways have I been living according to others' expectations rather than my own desires?

How can I better align my goals and aspirations with my core values to live a more authentic life?

"The most powerful relationship you will ever have is the relationship with yourself."

—Steve Maraboli

DAY 11

Date: ....

I am my own best friend and biggest supporter.

What self-care practices help me feel more connected and at peace with myself?

....
....
....
....
....
....
....
....
....

What actions can I take to nurture a loving and supportive relationship with myself?

....
....
....
....
....
....
....
....
....
....

"You yourself, as much as anybody in the entire universe, deserve your love and affection."

—Buddha

DAY 12

Date:

I am worthy of my own love, compassion, and respect, and I honor myself every day.

How can I show myself love and compassion today?

What steps can I take to prioritize my self-care and well-being?

"Loving yourself isn't vanity; it's sanity."

—Katrina Mayer

DAY 13

Date:

I love and respect myself deeply.

What does self-love mean to me, and how can I practice it daily?

How can I nurture a deeper sense of love and respect for myself?

"Self-acceptance is my refusal to be in an adversarial relationship with myself."

—Nathaniel Branden

DAY 14

Date:

I accept myself completely and unconditionally.

What steps can I take to move toward greater self-acceptance and peace with who I am?

What changes can I make to ensure that my self-talk is supportive, loving, and encouraging?

"What progress, you ask, have I made? I have begun to be a friend to myself."

—Seneca

DAY 15

Date:

I embrace my imperfections and appreciate the person I am becoming.

How do I respond to my own mistakes and failures, and what does it reveal about my relationship with myself?

How can I cultivate a more positive and supportive inner dialogue?

"The happiness of your life depends upon the quality of your thoughts."

—Marcus Aurelius

DAY 16

Date:

I cultivate a mindset that attracts joy, peace, and fulfillment.

What recurring negative thoughts do I need to address and transform?

How can I reframe negative thoughts into positive and constructive ones?

"He who learns but does not think is lost! He who thinks but does not learn is in great danger."

—Confucius

DAY 17

Date: _____

I think critically and apply my learning thoughtfully.

How can I balance learning and thinking to ensure effective personal growth?

_____
_____
_____
_____
_____
_____
_____
_____
_____
_____

What areas of my life could benefit from more thoughtful application of what I know to be true?

_____
_____
_____
_____
_____
_____
_____
_____
_____
_____
_____
_____

"Love yourself first and everything else falls into line."

—Lucille Ball

DAY 18

Date: _____

I am committed to understanding and loving myself more deeply each day.

What progress have I made in treating myself with the same love and respect that I offer to others?

_____
_____
_____
_____
_____
_____
_____
_____
_____

What boundaries do I need to set to protect my well-being and prioritize my relationship with myself?

_____
_____
_____
_____
_____
_____
_____
_____
_____
_____
_____

"Your beliefs become your thoughts, your thoughts become your words, your words become your actions, your actions become your habits, your habits become your values, your values become your destiny."

—Mahatma Gandhi

DAY 19

Date:

I live in alignment with my core values, and they bring me peace and fulfillment.

In what ways do my values contribute to my sense of purpose and fulfillment?

What are my core values, and how do they guide my decisions and actions? How aligned are my values, goals, and purpose?

"The privilege of a lifetime is to become who you truly are."

—Carl Jung

DAY 20

Date: ....

I celebrate my uniqueness and embrace who I am.

How can I celebrate and honor my unique qualities today?

What aspects of myself do I appreciate the most, and how can I acknowledge them more often?

"The more I read, the more I acquire, the more certain I am that I know nothing."

—Voltaire

DAY 21

Date:

I remain humble and open-minded, knowing there is always more to learn about everything, including myself.

How can I maintain humility and openness as I continue my learning journey?

What can I do today to embrace a beginner's mindset and welcome new knowledge?

"Everything you can imagine is real."

—Pablo Picasso

DAY 22

Date: _____

I am the creator of my own reality, and I joyfully bring my imagined visions to life.

In which ways can I better use my imagination to achieve the life I desire?

What steps can I take today to turn my wildest dreams into tangible realities?

"The more you know yourself, the more clarity there is."

—Jiddu Krishnamurti

DAY 23

Date:

I gain clarity through self-knowledge.

How has self-knowledge brought clarity to my life?

What aspects of myself need more clarity and understanding?

"Self-reflection is the school of wisdom."

—Baltasar Gracián

DAY 24

Date:

I embrace self-reflection as a powerful tool for cultivating wisdom and personal growth.

How has self-reflection contributed to my personal wisdom?

What insights or lessons have I gained through past moments of self-reflection, and how can I apply them moving forward?

"He who knows others is wise; he who knows himself is enlightened."

—Lao Tzu

DAY 25

Date:

I seek enlightenment through self-knowledge.

How has self-knowledge helped me to achieve my goals?

In what areas of my life do I feel I could benefit from deeper self-knowledge, and what steps can I take to incorporate it more intentionally?

"What we achieve inwardly will change outer reality."

—Plutarch

DAY 26

Date:

I explore my inner world with curiosity and openness.

How can I deepen my understanding of my inner self?

What can I do to cultivate a deeper connection with my inner wisdom and intuition?

"When I understand myself, I understand you, and out of that understanding comes love."

—Jiddu Krishnamurti

DAY 27

Date:

I celebrate my unique qualities and embrace all aspects of my being.

In what ways can I practice self-compassion and self-acceptance to enhance my ability to extend love and understanding to others?

How can I cultivate a mindset of curiosity and openness to truly understand the experiences and perspectives of those around me?

"The unexamined life is not worth living."

—Socrates

DAY 28

Date: _____

I examine my life to create meaning and purpose.

How do I respond to challenges or setbacks, and how might a deeper examination of my thoughts and actions lead to greater understanding?

_____
_____
_____
_____
_____
_____
_____
_____
_____

How can I deepen my practice of self-reflection to ensure that I am living in alignment with my values and aspirations?

_____
_____
_____
_____
_____
_____
_____
_____
_____
_____

Section 2:
OWNING

"You must take personal responsibility. You cannot change the circumstances, the seasons, or the wind, but you can change yourself."

—Jim Rohn

DAY 29

Date:

I take full ownership of my thoughts, emotions, and actions.

How can I cultivate a sense of accountability and self-reliance in order to create the life I desire?

What beliefs or habits do I need to let go of in order to take full ownership of my life and my future?

"The moment you take responsibility for everything in your life is the moment you can change anything in your life."

—Hal Elrod

DAY 30

Date:

I accept responsibility for my past, present, and future.

In what areas of my life am I currently avoiding taking responsibility, and why?

What small, intentional changes can I make today to align myself more closely with my values and the life I desire?

"For every minute you are angry you lose sixty seconds of happiness."

—Ralph Waldo Emerson

DAY 31

Date:

I release the need to blame others for my circumstances.

To whom and in what situations do I give my joy away?

How can I reframe challenging situations to find opportunities for growth and gratitude instead of anger, fear, or resentment?

"You are not a product of your circumstances, but a product of your decisions."

—Stephen Covey

DAY 32

Date: _____

I have the power to create positive change in my life.

What small changes can I make today to take control of my life?

_____
_____
_____
_____
_____
_____
_____
_____
_____
_____

How can I reclaim my power and agency in areas where I feel powerless?

_____
_____
_____
_____
_____
_____
_____
_____
_____
_____
_____

"You become what you give your attention to. If you yourself don't choose what thoughts and images you expose yourself to, someone else will."

—Epictetus

DAY 33

Date: _____

I am the gatekeeper of my mind, carefully selecting what influences I allow in.

How does the content I'm exposed to and regularly consume contribute to my growth and overall mental state?

What steps can I take today to reclaim my power over my attention and align it with my values and aspirations?

"Happiness and freedom begin with a clear understanding of one principle: Some things are within our control, and some things are not."

—Epictetus

DAY 34

Date:

I focus on what I can control and release what I cannot.

What are some areas of my life where I need to practice more serenity and acceptance of the things I cannot change?

How can I better focus my energy and time on what I can change?

> *"It is not in the stars to hold our destiny but in ourselves."*
>
> —William Shakespeare

DAY 35

Date:

I am the creator of my own destiny.

In what ways can I take full responsibility for my current circumstances?

How can I live my life from a place of ownership and empowerment?

"With great power there must also come great responsibility."

—V<small>OLTAIRE</small>

DAY 36

Date:

I take full responsibility for my actions and their consequences.

How can I better manage my power and responsibilities to achieve my goals?

What areas of my life require more accountability and commitment from me?

"The key is to keep company only with people who uplift you, whose presence calls forth your best."

—Ralph Waldo Emerson

DAY 37

Date:

I deserve relationships that respect and honor my boundaries.

Who are my destiny helpers?

In what ways can I show appreciation and nurture the relationships that positively impact my life?

"*Act as if what you do makes a difference. It does.*"

—William James

DAY 38

Date:

My actions have a meaningful impact on my life and the lives of others.

How can I use my actions to positively influence those around me?

What changes can I make in my mindset and behavior to amplify the difference I wish to see in the world?

"Responsibility is the price of freedom."

—Elbert Hubbard

DAY 39

Date:

I am free to choose my path and take responsibility for my choices.

How does taking responsibility for my life contribute to my sense of freedom?

How can I balance personal responsibility with the need for self-care and compassion?

"The greatest glory in living lies not in never falling, but in rising every time we fall."

—Nelson Mandela

DAY 40

Date:

I embrace failure as a steppingstone to success.

How have past failures contributed to my growth and success?

How can I reframe my failures to see them as opportunities for growth?

"Don't watch the clock; do what it does. Keep going."

—Sam Levenson

DAY 41

Date:

I persistently move forward, regardless of the challenges I face.

How can I keep myself motivated and moving forward during challenging times?

What strategies can I use to maintain momentum and progress?

*"If you can dream it,
you can do it."*

—Walt Disney

DAY 42

Date: ....

I believe in my dreams and my ability to achieve them.

How can I nurture my dreams and keep them alive in my daily life?

What actions can I take today to bring my dreams closer to reality?

"What lies behind us and what lies before us are tiny matters compared to what lies within us."

—Ralph Waldo Emerson

DAY 43

Date:

I have the inner strength and resources to overcome any challenge.

How can I draw upon my inner strength in times of adversity?

What inner qualities can I cultivate to better handle life's challenges?

"Success is not the key to happiness. Happiness is the key to success. If you love what you are doing, you will be successful."

—Albert Schweitzer

DAY 44

Date:

I find joy and fulfillment in my pursuits, knowing that happiness leads to success.

How can I ensure that my pursuits bring me joy and fulfillment?

What activities or goals make me genuinely happy, and how can I incorporate more of them into my life?

"We are what we repeatedly do. Excellence, then, is not an act, but a habit."

—Aristotle

DAY 45

Date:

I cultivate excellence through my daily habits and actions.

Which habits have contributed to my growth and excellence?

What new habits can I develop to enhance my personal and professional growth?

"The best way to predict the future is to create it."

—Peter Drucker

DAY 46

Date:

I actively create the future I desire through my actions today.

How can I take control of my future by making deliberate choices today?

What steps can I take now to shape the future I envision for myself?

"Your life does not get better by chance; it gets better by change."

—Jim Rohn

DAY 47

Date:

I embrace change as a pathway to a better life.

How can I welcome and adapt to changes in my life to improve it?

What internal beliefs do I need to change to take on challenges more positively?

"We all have possibilities we don't know about. We can do things we don't even dream we can do."

—Dale Carnegie

DAY 48

Date:

My potential is limitless, and I release any self-imposed limitations.

What self-imposed limitations must I release to achieve my full potential?

How can I expand my thinking to encourage and embrace greater possibilities?

"*Your task is not to foresee the future, but to enable it.*"

—Antoine de Saint-Exupéry

DAY 49

Date:

I create a future aligned with my values and dreams.

How can I actively shape my future daily?

What actions can I take now to enable the future I desire?

"Believe you can and you're halfway there."

—Theodore Roosevelt

DAY 50

Date: ....

I believe in myself, my power within and my ability to achieve my goals.

How can I strengthen my belief in my abilities?

How can I build greater self-confidence to pursue my goals?

"The power to question is the basis of all human progress."

—Indira Gandhi

DAY 51

Date:

I ask questions that lead to deeper understanding and growth.

What questions can I ask myself to gain new insights?

How can I cultivate a habit of asking powerful, transformative questions?

"*We acquire the strength we have overcome.*"

—Ralph Waldo Emerson

DAY 52

Date: _____

I acknowledge my strengths and celebrate them without comparison to others.

Reflecting on past challenges, what strengths did I discover within myself that helped me overcome them?

_____
_____
_____
_____
_____
_____
_____
_____
_____

What perceived weaknesses can I turn into strengths through acceptance and effort?

_____
_____
_____
_____
_____
_____
_____
_____
_____
_____

"In the middle of difficulty lies opportunity."

—Albert Einstein

DAY 53

Date:

I find opportunities for growth in every challenge.

How can I turn current challenges into opportunities for growth?

What difficulties am I facing, and how can I reframe them as opportunities?

Section 3:
VALIDATION

"I am the master of my fate; I am the captain of my soul."

—William Ernest Henley

DAY 54

Date:

I am freedom.

Reflect on a time when you felt most in control of your life. What mindset or actions contributed to that sense of empowerment?

In which areas of my life have I taken a back seat and relinquished my position as the driver of my life?

"Your value doesn't decrease based on someone's inability to see your worth."

—U̲nknown

DAY 55

Date:

I am worthy of love, respect, and happiness just as I am.

How can I validate and affirm myself today?

What beliefs about myself do I need to let go of, in order to fully embrace who I am?

"You alone are enough. You have nothing to prove to anybody."

—Maya Angelou

DAY 56

Date:

I am enough.

How does the belief that "I am enough" change the way I approach challenges and interactions with others?

How can I cultivate a mindset of self-acceptance and self-love, regardless of the presence or absence of external validation?

"The privilege of a lifetime is being who you are."

—Joseph Campbell

DAY 57

Date:

I attract relationships that bring out the best in me.

Who in my life consistently uplifts and inspires me?

What aspects of myself do I appreciate the most, and how can I acknowledge them more often?

"Stop looking outside for scraps of validation; you have within you an infinite source of love."

—Rumi

DAY 58

Date:

I honor and value my authentic self.

How can I embrace my true self more fully today?

In what aspects of my identity have I been seeking the approval of others and how can I approve myself instead?

"Number one in your life's blueprint should be a deep belief in your own dignity, your worth, and your own somebodiness. Don't allow anybody to make you feel that you're nobody. Always feel that you count. Always feel that you have worth, and always feel that your life has ultimate significance."

—Martin Luther King Jr.

DAY 59

Date:

I am somebody.

In what ways do I allow others to dictate my sense of worth and significance?

Reflecting on the significance of my life and the impact I have on others, how does recognizing my ultimate significance influence my actions and decisions?

"You are very powerful, provided you know how powerful you are."

—Yogi Bhajan

DAY 60

Date:

I recognize and embrace my inner power.

How can I harness my inner strength to overcome challenges?

How can I remind myself of my inner power and worth in both good and difficult times?

"Associate with those who will make a better person of you. Welcome those whom you yourself can improve. The process is mutual; for people learn while they teach."

—Seneca

DAY 61

Date:

I attract relationships that bring out the best in me.

How can I actively seek out and cultivate relationships that enhance my well-being and personal development?

How do I discern which relationships are truly mutual—and which ones I've outgrown?

"Self-worth comes from one thing—thinking that you are worthy."

—Wayne Dyer

DAY 62

Date:

I am inherently worthy, simply by being myself.

How can I reinforce my sense of self-worth today?

What actions can I take to honor my own worthiness?

"True happiness is to enjoy the present, without anxious dependence upon the future."

—Seneca

DAY 63

Date:

I enjoy now.

How can I reinforce my sense of happiness today?

How can I shift my focus from anxiously anticipating the future to fully embracing the opportunities and experiences available to me right now?

"Be faithful to that which exists within yourself."

—André Gide

DAY 64

Date:

I honor my values.

Which of my values do I need to honor more?

What values are most important to me, and how can I live and stay true to them more fully?

"To thine own self be true."

—William Shakespeare

DAY 65

Date:

I trust and follow my North Star.

How can I stay true to myself in every situation?

What does my life look like when I'm being true to and truthful with myself?

*"You are you. Now,
isn't that pleasant?"*

—Dr. Seuss

DAY 66

Date:

I find joy and contentment in being authentically myself.

How do I feel when I am most authentically myself, and what environments or activities encourage this authenticity?

How can I show up daily as who I truly am?

Section 4:
EXPANSION

"Life begins at the end of your comfort zone."

—Neale Donald Walsch

DAY 67

Date:

I welcome change and growth as opportunities for expansion.

What small step can I take today to step out of my comfort zone?

How can I cultivate a mindset of abundance and possibility in my life?

"The only way to make sense out of change is to plunge into it, move with it, and join the dance."

—A<small>LAN</small> W<small>ATTS</small>

DAY 68

Date:

I am adaptable and open to the flow of life.

How can I embrace change as a natural part of life?

What opportunities for growth and expansion are present in my life today?

"The only constant in life is change."

—Heraclitus

DAY 68

Date:

I am adaptable and open to the flow of life.

How can I embrace change as a natural part of life?

What opportunities for growth and expansion are present in my life today?

"The only constant in life is change."

—Heraclitus

DAY 69

Date: ....

I trust that everything is unfolding for my highest good.

How can I surrender to the flow of life and trust in the universe's plan for me?

....
....
....
....
....
....
....
....
....

Considering how often I find myself worrying about the future, how does this impact my ability to enjoy the present?

....
....
....
....
....
....
....
....
....
....
....
....

"It is not because things are difficult that we do not dare; it is because we do not dare that they are difficult."

—Seneca

DAY 70

Date: _____

I can achieve my goals and dreams.

Which stretch goals can I set to move beyond my comfort zone today?

_____
_____
_____
_____
_____
_____
_____
_____

What would my life look like if I stepped into my fullest potential and lived authentically?

_____
_____
_____
_____
_____
_____
_____
_____
_____
_____

"Progress is impossible without change, and those who cannot change their minds cannot change anything."

—George Bernard Shaw

DAY 71

Date:

I am constantly evolving and expanding my consciousness.

What beliefs or habits do I need to let go of for the emergence of my higher self?

How can I align my actions with my highest ideals and aspirations?

"Life is inherently risky. There is only one big risk you should avoid at all costs, and that is the risk of doing nothing."

—Denis Waitley

DAY 72

Date:

I welcome new experiences and opportunities with enthusiasm.

What risks am I willing to take in order to grow and expand?

How can I cultivate a sense of purpose and meaning that transcends external achievements?

"Go confidently in the direction of your dreams. Live the life you have imagined."

—Henry David Thoreau

DAY 73

Date:

I am grateful for the journey of self-discovery and growth.

What steps can I take today to move closer to my dreams?

....
....
....
....
....
....
....
....
....

What legacy do I want to leave behind, and how can I start living in alignment with that vision today?

....
....
....
....
....
....
....
....
....
....
....

"The only way to achieve the impossible is to believe it is possible."

—Charles Kingsleigh

DAY 74

Date:

I believe in my ability to create positive change in my life.

What have I learned about myself from the obstacles I have overcome in the past?

How can I transform my fear of failure into a catalyst for change and action?

"Life in abundance comes only through great love."

—Elbert Hubbard

DAY 75

Date:

My capacity for love knows no bounds, and it leads me to a life filled with joy, connection, and purpose.

What does "great love" mean to me, and how does it contribute to a sense of abundance in my life?

How can I extend love and kindness to myself and others, creating a ripple effect of abundance and joy in my world?

"The man who moves a mountain begins by carrying away small stones."

—Confucius

DAY 76

Date: _____

I achieve my goals through consistent and dedicated effort.

What small, manageable steps can I take today toward my larger goals?

....
....
....
....
....
....
....
....
....
....

How can I break down my long-term goals into actionable, daily tasks?

....
....
....
....
....
....
....
....
....
....
....

"An investment in knowledge pays the best interest."

—Benjamin Franklin

DAY 77

Date:

I invest in my growth by continuously expanding my knowledge and skills.

What investments in learning have benefited my goals?

How can I prioritize and make time for learning in service of my desired future self?

> "Life is either a daring adventure or nothing at all."
>
> —Helen Keller

DAY 78

Date:

I embrace new experiences and opportunities with courage and enthusiasm.

What new experiences or opportunities can I embrace to expand my horizons?

What are the steps I need to take to step out of my comfort zone today to foster personal growth?

"It always seems impossible until it's done."

—Nelson Mandela

DAY 79

Date:

I am capable of achieving more than I ever thought possible.

What limitations have I placed on myself, and how can I push beyond them?

What bold steps can I take to challenge my perceived limitations?

"Do not go where the path may lead, go instead where there is no path and leave a trail."

—Ralph Waldo Emerson

DAY 80

Date:

I forge my own path and create my own unique journey.

How can I create my own path instead of letting others choose for me?

What innovative or unconventional approaches can I take to achieve my goals?

"Man cannot discover new oceans unless he has the courage to lose sight of the shore."

—André Gide

DAY 81

Date:

I have the courage to explore new possibilities and adventures.

What new opportunities can I explore to expand my understanding of the world?

How can I cultivate the courage to venture into the unknown?

"The only limit to our realization of tomorrow is our doubts of today."

—Franklin D. Roosevelt

DAY 82

Date: ....

I release doubt and embrace the limitless possibilities of my future.

How can I overcome doubts that hold me back from achieving my full potential?

....
....
....
....
....
....
....
....
....
....
....
....

What mindset shifts can I make to embrace a future filled with limitless possibilities?

....
....
....
....
....
....
....
....
....
....
....
....

"Don't be afraid to give up the good to go for the great."

—John D. Rockefeller

DAY 83

Date: ....

I let go of the good to make room for the great.

What good things in my life might be holding me back from achieving greatness?

....
....
....
....
....
....
....
....
....
....

How can I create space in my life for greater opportunities and experiences?

....
....
....
....
....
....
....
....
....
....
....
....

"You miss 100% of the shots you don't take."

—Wayne Gretzky

DAY 84

Date:

I take bold steps toward my goals, knowing that each step brings me closer to success.

What bold step can I take today toward my goals?

What opportunities am I missing by not taking action, and how can I change that today?

"The secret of getting ahead is getting started."

—Mark Twain

DAY 85

Date:

I begin each journey with confidence and an open heart.

What journey have I been hesitant to start, and why?

What can I do today to take the first step on this new journey?

"It is never too late to be what you might have been."

—George Eliot

DAY 86

Date:

It is never too late to pursue my true passions and goals.

What passions or goals have I put aside, and how can I revisit them?

How can I reignite my passion for the goals I once set aside?

"Twenty years from now you will be more disappointed by the things you didn't do than by the ones you did do."

—H. Jackson Brown Jr.

DAY 87

Date:

I take risks and seize opportunities to avoid future regrets.

What opportunities have I been hesitant to take, and why?

What is one opportunity I can seize today to avoid future regret?

"You must do the thing you think you cannot do."

—Eleanor Roosevelt

DAY 88

Date:

I face my fears and tackle challenges head-on.

What fears are holding me back, and how can I confront them?

What challenging task can I take on today to prove my capabilities?

"Life shrinks or expands in proportion to one's courage."

—Anaïs Nin

DAY 89

Date:

I expand my life by living courageously.

How has courage helped me expand my life?

In which areas of my life do I need more courage?

"The journey of a thousand miles begins with one step."

—Lao Tzu

DAY 90

Date: _____

I celebrate my journey and the steps I have taken toward self-discovery.

How have the steps I have taken over the past 90 days transformed me?

_____
_____
_____
_____
_____
_____
_____
_____
_____

What have I learned from this journey, and how will I continue to grow, expand, and evolve?

_____
_____
_____
_____
_____
_____
_____
_____
_____
_____
_____
_____

Congratulations on completing
your 90-day journey of self-discovery with LOVE.

Integration and Insights:

- Reflect on the insights gained from the past 90-day journey.
- What have been the most significant lessons learned during this time about yourself?
- How have these insights impacted your self-discovery journey so far?
- How has your understanding of self-love evolved throughout this journey?
- What changes would you like to make as you continue forward?
- Review your affirmations, reflections, and powerful questions.
- Set intentions for how you will continue to apply the principles of learning, owning, validating, and expanding yourself in your life moving forward.

As you continue your path to transformation, remember to integrate the lessons learned and insights gained into your daily life.

May you continue to grow, expand, and embrace the journey of self-discovery with love and compassion.

Your story belongs to you. Own it!

www.ingramcontent.com/pod-product-compliance
Lightning Source LLC
Chambersburg PA
CBRC090220100526
44582CB00017B/198/J